Scripture Power

Helping Kids Love the Scriptures

DeNNiS A. WRight, PH.D.

BOOKCRAFT
SALT LAKE CITY, UTAH

For my wife, Kaye, and our wonderful married kids, Elise and Reid, Whitney and Andy, Geoffrey and Leah—and for those still at home, Stephen and Kimberly.

Not to forget the next generation, Kayla, Camille, Nathan, Hannah, Hailey, and the many more grandchildren to come. Kaye and I are so grateful for the wonderful blessing our family is to us.

Library of Congress Cataloging-in-Publication Data

Wright, Dennis A.
    Scripture power / Dennis A. Wright.
        p.   cm.
    ISBN 1-57008-831-4 (pbk.)
    1. Family—Religious life.   2. Christian education of children.   3. Mormon Church—Doctrines.   4. Church of Jesus Christ of Latter-day Saints—Doctrines. 5. Bible—Reading.   I. Title
BX8643.F3 W75 2002
249—dc21   2002005444

Printed in the United States of America   72076-6963
Publishers Printing, Salt Lake City, UT

10   9   8   7   6   5   4   3   2   1

Contents

Foreword   v

Preface   ix

Acknowledgments   xi

1. Introduction   1

2. Growing Up with the Scriptures   7

3. Lap Time
   Birth to Two:
   Scripture Learning Begins   15

4. Story Time
   Three to Five:
   First Scripture Adventures   27

5. Play Time
   Six to Eleven:
   Having Fun with Scriptures   41

6. Teaching Time
   Twelve to Eighteen:
   Learning from the Scriptures   65

Index   83

Foreword

T his book is a must for parents or grandparents who
love the Lord, love the scriptures, and love children.
Consider the advantages of a child who has become
acquainted with the word of God and the promised blessings and good feelings associated with the scriptures.

Having been a teacher of children, and knowing the
challenge of holding their attention while increasing their
comprehension, I became excited about the contents of this
book. I find that it presents a useful way to help children
develop confidence in finding answers in the scriptures
while also building strong family relationships. Children are
receptive to the things of the Spirit when they are presented
in a way suited to their abilities and interests. By using the
great ideas provided in this book, parents can help their
children come to love the scriptures. The benefits of familiarity with scripture stories and principles—such as choice,

accountability, and obedience—will provide protection in this challenging world that endangers our youth.

While many do not learn to love the scriptures as children, it appears evident to me that by using the guidelines, activities, and experiences presented by Brother Wright, this need not be so. No time must be lost in preparing youth with strong testimonies for the challenging times ahead.

Preparation for a mission does not begin in the clothing store two weeks before entering the Missionary Training Center. It begins in the nursery. And as this book explains, even the sound of the mother's voice reading the scriptures establishes a familiarity with the sounds of the word of God, giving children an added advantage as they mature in the gospel.

I see the use of this book for teaching children of all ages, from cradle to mission, like the hub of a wheel. Every activity reaches out from the center core of the scriptures. The book is wisely and cleverly developmental in using singing, drama, art, visual aids, games, language, and communication skills to build understanding. These things can help children learn to use the scriptures to ask questions, find answers, express insights, and share feelings in a family setting.

The book's style is comfortable for the least experienced teacher, and the content is applicable to the most knowledgeable. The guidelines are reasonable in both time and experience. Having been in the Wright home and seen the relationship between parents and children and their love for and familiarity with the scriptures, I believe that this book presents a tried-and-true approach.

Today it is customary—and for some parents it seems

essential—to enroll children in early preschool even before kindergarten so they will keep pace with the opportunities to learn. Consider the many benefits for children who are enrolled in family activities that open the scriptures in exciting ways to their young minds. The curriculum is unquestionably worthwhile; it has been with us for thousands of years. The most effective teachers are parents, and our need for them is perhaps greater than in any time past.

ARDETH GREENE KAPP

PreFace

I suppose it is important that you know a grandpa is writing this book. At this time in our life Kaye and I have five children, two sons-in-law, a daughter-in-law, and five beautiful grandchildren. Our married children are busy with young children and demanding careers and church service. Our returned missionary son is busy with school, and our youngest daughter is entering her first year of college.

What a blessing it was to see our daughters sealed to righteous young men and our sons serve faithfully as missionaries. We are grateful that our children have embraced the gospel, and we are excited about our new role as grandparents. This time of life does bring a greater appreciation for family.

It has taken me this long to understand something about children and the scriptures. It is not that I haven't thought about the topic; it just takes experience to understand how it works. I wish I had known about the ideas in this book earlier in our family life, but I had to learn from my own successes and failures and by watching others. I am grateful that I did some things right, for our children do read and enjoy the scriptures. But in writing this book, I recognize that we could have given our children more help.

Maybe that is why I wrote this book. Most parents love the scriptures and want to share them with their children, but they don't always know how. Experience with my family has taught me that reading for a few minutes every day is not enough. Because I wanted to encourage my children to understand and appreciate the scriptures, I experimented with different ideas and activities. Kaye and I found that our children became more interested in the scriptures when we used a variety of approaches. This book provides the ideas and suggestions that we found useful in moving beyond a routine approach to the scriptures. Of course, not all the ideas are completely original, as much of what I know comes from learning from the experiences of others.

The book begins with an introduction and then provides an overview of the ways children develop in their understanding and appreciation of the scriptures. As part of the introduction, I suggest five developmental stages that provide us with unique opportunities to encourage a love of the scriptures. The remaining chapters describe each stage more completely and suggest practical ideas that encourage an interest in the scriptures.

I hope you find this book to be a practical resource as you create experiences that help your children understand and appreciate the scriptures. I know you will be grateful you made the effort as you see your children develop confidence in the word of God.

AcKNoWLedgMeNtS

I am grateful for my mother, who first shared scripture sto-ries with me. Her anchor of faith has greatly blessed my life.

This book was possible because of the examples shared by so many friends and neighbors through the years. Casey Nelson, a student research assistant, is responsible for the artwork. She is such a talented illustrator. My editor, Jack Lyon, has been most helpful and appreciated in the process of refining the manuscript.

CHAPTER 1

Introduction

Not all of our young people can read and understand the scriptures. Those who are successful often come from homes in which a special effort has been made to provide regular scripture experiences for the children.

Our home was unusually quiet as I arrived home from a busy day at work. I was tired because the week had been an exhausting one as we prepared for a missionary farewell, visited with family guests, and helped our son, Stephen, prepare for his mission. The guests were now gone, we had completed the necessary preparations, and the next day our family would take Stephen to the Missionary Training Center.

I walked through the house, calling to see if anyone was home. The upstairs was empty, so I went downstairs where I knew Stephen had been packing for his adventure. Three bulging bags sat in the middle of the floor. His packing was done. Continuing down the hall, I found Stephen sitting at his desk, intently studying the Book of Mormon.

The scene made me remember his first Book of Mormon. It seemed like only yesterday that Stephen received a personal copy with his name stamped in gold on the cover. Our mission president had given this gift with the promise that this new member of our family would grow up with a testimony of the truthfulness of the book.

In the years that followed, we did all we could to encourage Stephen and the rest of our children to rely on the scriptures as a source of personal strength. I thought of the many family home evenings and other special times in which the scriptures played an important part. I remembered the times we read together and talked about the ideas revealed in the scriptures.

As I watched my son read, I was grateful that we had made an effort and that the promise had been fulfilled. Our attempts to encourage our son to develop confidence in the scriptures had been successful. It was now his turn to help others discover the truthfulness of the word of God.

My first experience with young people who love the scriptures came early in my career as a seminary teacher. Faced with a class of high school sophomores, I quickly realized that there was a wide range in their scripture-reading ability and interest. I was curious about why many students read aloud from the scriptures with few problems but did not seem to understand what they read. I had assumed that they would be able to understand the ideas if they could read the words, but I was surprised to discover that this was not always the case.

Randy enjoyed the scriptures. When questioned after

reading, he could provide thoughtful answers and ideas. He was not unique as there were many other students who also demonstrated the ability to understand the scriptures. I wondered why these students seemed to be comfortable with the scriptures while others struggled to understand what they read.

I wanted to find out more about this problem. Observing my students, I learned that those who were at ease reading the scriptures were not necessarily brighter or more capable than other students. They were unique only in the confidence they exhibited when asked to learn from the scriptures. So, in an effort to discover more about student differences in reading the scriptures, I put my graduate training to work and designed a small research project. It was no surprise when the results of this research demonstrated that children who could read and understand the scriptures came from families who regularly read and talked about them.

As a father of a young family, I wanted to know how I could provide this advantage for my children. During the years that followed, I asked questions and gathered as much information as I could about the families of students who loved the scriptures. I was not always successful in providing my own children with the experiences I had observed in others, but my children did receive sufficient help to develop confidence in the scriptures.

I wrote this book to share what I have learned about children and scriptures. As a grandpa, I am doing this so that those who are interested can have a resource to help them provide a heritage of rich scripture experiences for their families.

Where Do We Start?

Children and scriptures make a perfect match. Our children's natural desire to learn of Heavenly Father is satisfied in the stories and teachings of the scriptures. Their faith and testimony will grow as the Spirit teaches them the truthfulness of the gospel message. There is no better time to foster a love for the scriptures than during the early years when children are most ready and eager to learn.

A love for the scriptures provides a foundation that will keep our children secure in a confusing world. This book provides ideas that will help you develop within your children a love for the scriptures. It is not only about teaching your children to love reading, but more specifically it is about teaching your children to love reading and pondering the *scriptures*. The ideas presented in this book will bless your children by increasing their confidence in using the scriptures as a source of understanding and inspiration. My hope is that all children can grow up loving the scriptures and knowing of their truthfulness. While this may require real diligence on our part, the benefits are well worth the effort.

What Challenges Do We Face?

Parents face some real challenges in balancing life's demands. As we seek to help our children become comfortable with the scriptures, the following are important considerations.

First, there never seems to be enough time. One of our married daughters and her husband found that starting a home and a new career was most difficult and demanded a great deal of time. This reality, combined with Church and school responsibilities, left little extra time to read scriptures with their children. They determined that they would carefully plan to spend time reading the scriptures and emphasizing them during family home evening. There were some things they didn't have time for, but helping their children with the scriptures was always a priority.

Limited time should not be an insurmountable problem. While we all want to make time for children, these opportunities do not magically appear. As parents we must decide what should be done and the best time to do it. We must plan for, look for, and pray for time to teach our children from the scriptures.

Second, most parents are not professional teachers. My friend Linda questioned her own ability when I shared some ideas about helping children learn from the scriptures. "How can I ever do what you do?" she asked. "I'm not a teacher!" She worried that her work as a bank teller had not prepared her to help her children with the scriptures.

Linda found that she did not need special skills or materials to succeed. After considering a few practical ideas, such as those found in this book, and with her own love for her children, she was successful in providing scripture experiences for them.

Third, most families have children with different needs. Our friends the Thompsons have five children of different ages, each with unique needs. This made for an interesting teaching challenge. They learned that one important factor in helping their children learn from the scriptures depended on their understanding of how children develop and how parents can help them learn at each stage in their development.

In the next chapter you will find a description of the stages of child development and how each relates to scripture learning. Each stage presents a unique opportunity. Understanding the stages will help you take advantage of them to encourage scripture learning. As you consider these stages, think of your own children and how you can better help them with the scriptures.

Summary

Much can be done to help our children develop an appreciation for the scriptures. You will need to overcome the challenges of limited time and individual differences. However real these challenges may be, parents who commit themselves to this most important effort can do much to help their children. Among the many ideas and resources in this book, you will find many useful ways to instill in your children a love for the scriptures.

Children can develop a love for the scriptures. When they grow up with the scriptures, they gain confidence in them as a source of learning and strength. That is why I wrote this book. It contains practical ideas gathered from families who have succeeded in helping their children love the word of the Lord.

CHAPTER 2

GroWiNg Up WitH the Scriptures

Children gradually learn to understand and appreciate
the scriptures. At each point in their development
they experience the scriptures at a different level of
complexity and understanding. Each stage suggests different
teaching opportunities appropriate to children's abilities.

On a Monday night long ago, I tried to gather my family
into the living room for our regular home evening. Our
teenager, Elise, was on the phone, while our twelve-year-
old, Whitney, dutifully reminded everyone that it was time
to start. Geoffrey, age ten, bounced his Chicago Bulls basketball on the floor, much to the irritation of his sisters,
while our eight-year-old, Stephen, attacked the sofa cush-
ions with his G.I. Joe. Kimberly, our youngest, cuddled next
to her mother, waiting patiently for the evening activity to
begin. I wondered if it would be possible to present a lesson
that would meet the different needs in our family that night.
But planning scripture experiences for our families is not as

complicated as I once thought when we understand children and how they develop.

Children Are Constantly Changing

Children pass through certain stages as they develop physically, mentally, socially, emotionally, and spiritually. Each stage presents a unique opportunity to teach them from the scriptures. Scripture experiences over time have a cumulative effect as your children enjoy the scriptures as a source of strength and encouragement. If you understand how children develop, you can better provide experiences appropriate for their abilities.

During the first stage (ages birth to two), infants and toddlers are dependent and learn best through listening and observing.

As they grow, children enter the second stage (ages three to five) and begin to use language for entertainment and learning.

In the third stage (ages six to eleven) play becomes an important part of learning as children demonstrate increased independence.

During the fourth stage (ages twelve to eighteen), direct teaching becomes productive when children develop formal learning skills. As reading skills mature, parents play a less directive role because children can explore for themselves the power of the scriptures.

The following brief descriptions summarize the behaviors and attitudes characteristic of each stage of development. Of course, children develop at different rates and in unique ways, and you should not use these descriptions to compare children or judge maturity levels. Rather, you should use them to think about how best to help your children grow to love the scriptures.

Stage One: Lap Time (Birth to Two)—Scripture Learning Begins

From the time they are born until the age of two, children learn language basics. They listen, imitate, and experiment in developing their communication skills. This gives parents the opportunity to introduce the special language of the scriptures. Becoming familiar with the particular sounds and rhythms of scriptural language at an early age provides a foundation for later learning. During this stage parents cuddle their children while reading aloud from the scriptures. Such experiences are valuable because they link scriptural language with the love and attention of the parents. This intimate experience makes this an important time.

Stage Two: Story Time (Three to Five)—First Scripture Adventures

Beginning language and reading skills develop significantly from ages three to five. During this time children become fluent with language. They also become aware of the purpose of a book and how to use it for pleasure and information. They begin to understand the relationship of printed words to speech and realize that words and pictures go together. Scripture storybooks become important. Children love looking at pictures and enjoy hearing their favorite stories over and over again. During this stage you can read from picture books and storybooks to complement continued reading of the scriptures. This will result in increased understanding of both scripture content and language.

Stage Three: Play Time (Six to Eleven)—Fun with the Scriptures

Children from six to eleven need to be active. They run, jump, ride, and play with great enthusiasm and energy. With their short attention spans, they explore the world with their new skills. During this stage children begin to understand what is right and wrong and are anxious to please and be accepted by teachers and parents. It is during this age that they experience significant growth in their personal faith and testimony.

Scripture games and activities are effective during this stage as children's growing independence and skill enable them to enjoy new challenges. Scripture understanding is developed through activities that reinforce story details, teach values and principles, and provide new insights and applications. It is during this stage that family home evening provides a great opportunity for scripture learning.

Stage Four: Teaching Time (Twelve to Eighteen)— Learning from the Scriptures

Young people from twelve to eighteen develop skills that make formal learning effective. They become more independent in scripture learning as their attention spans increase and their reading skills mature. They can learn for themselves the gospel principles taught in the scriptures. This can be a challenge as young readers encounter unusual words and phrases that make passages difficult to understand. To prevent these difficulties from discouraging reading independence, parents and teachers need to help and encourage young readers.

They can do this through formal teaching opportunities

in family home evening, seminary, and Sunday classes. It is also important to encourage gospel-centered discussions that give youth an opportunity to express opinions and beliefs gained from their reading and study. During this stage regular independent reading becomes important as youth personalize habits of regular scripture study.

The challenges faced by our teen-aged youth often give us an opportunity to help them understand the personal relevance of the scriptures. As youth mature they can better understand the meaning of scripture passages. While they have sufficient skills to be independent in scripture learning, they may be insufficiently mature to take advantage of their new abilities. With our encouragement, they can develop an increasing love and appreciation for the scriptures. It does require patience and vision on the part of supportive parents, but it is worth the effort.

Summary

This chapter introduced the importance of growing up with the scriptures and the role of parents at each stage of children's development. First it is important to introduce the language of the scriptures, share wonderful stories, and play games that reinforce learning. Later, formal instruction becomes important in developing a greater understanding and appreciation of the scriptures.

It is not easy to find time to meet a variety of family needs and know how to best help your children. I am grateful that children come to this life with a desire to learn about their Heavenly Father and seem naturally drawn to his word. Once we recognize the importance of the scriptures for our children, we start on a path that will bless their lives in the years to come.

Don't forget that you, as a parent, are uniquely qualified to help your children develop a love for the scriptures. You are directly involved in the most receptive time of your children's lives, and what you do for them will influence their lifelong attitudes and habits. The natural love and care you provide create a personalized learning environment perfect for your children. Learning to love the scriptures is a natural outgrowth of doing a few simple things that only parents can do best.

Developmental Stages of Scripture Learning

Stage	Characteristics	Opportunities
1. Lap time: ages birth to two	Children develop prereading skills through listening, imitation, and experimentation.	Introduce the unique language of the scriptures through reading aloud.
2. Story time: ages three to five	Children develop an awareness of books and their purpose. Children are especially interested in stories and pictures.	Provide a wide variety of picture books related to the scriptures. Reading aloud remains important.
3. Play Time: ages six to eleven	Children learn best through doing. Growing independence enables them to participate in a wide range of learning activities	Listen to children read and encourage related discussion Create an opportunity for children to use reading skills in games or activities that promote learning.
4. Teaching time: ages twelve to eighteen	Children develop thinking skills and independent learning. Testimony becomes a personal experience.	Provide opportunities to use the scriptures in practical ways related to personal life or church service. Listen more and allow youth to explore their responses to the scriptures.

CHAPTER 3

Lap Time

Birth to Two: Scripture Learning Begins

My grandchildren are learning to love the scriptures as they snuggle in their parents' arms and listen to the soothing language of the scriptures. Scripture reading should begin at birth when the language of the scriptures can be introduced in an environment rich in love and acceptance. If you will read the scriptures with your children from birth, you will teach them to take comfort in the language of the scriptures. For them it will not be a strange or challenging language but a natural part of their life.

The rocking chair was an important part of our family's first home. My wife and I spent wonderful hours in the rocker becoming acquainted with each of our five children. It was in this chair that our children first experienced the word of God. It seemed such a natural thing to cuddle each new infant and read aloud to him or her from one of our standard works. Because of this, our children's first awareness of the scriptures became inseparably linked to rocking-chair memories.

Lap-time experiences with the scriptures begin at birth and continue throughout childhood. It is during the first two years that the foundation for later scripture learning is established. Sitting in the rocking chair, I would pick up the scriptures and read aloud while holding one of our children. This seemed such a natural thing to do. The time I spent reading aloud was not long. I never thought it had to be; regularly reading a little bit seemed to work best. While I most enjoyed reading to our children from the Book of Mormon, I also read from different scriptures to provide variety for me as a reader as well for my children.

A lap-time experience with the scriptures is natural and simple. There is no need to wait until an infant reaches a certain age. Lap-time scripture reading can begin the first day of life. Some mothers read aloud while feeding their babies; others prefer a different time. I don't think there is a single best time or place for everyone, but several important constants do exist. The place must be comfortable for both infant and parent. A special blanket, stuffed toys, or other favorite things can also help a child enjoy the experience. Try reading with a soft, comforting voice; the soothing sound helps establish an environment of learning and nurturing.

Of course, sometimes attempts at lap-time reading will fail. In spite of our best efforts, our infants will not always cooperate, making flexibility and patience essential. Success will come over time rather than in one experience.

But why is the lap-time experience so important in

developing children's love for and understanding of the scriptures? I think it is related to language development.

The Importance of the Lap-Time Experience

Church members commonly complain that the language of the scriptures is difficult to understand. Many dislike the unusual grammar and wording, and the scriptures do present unique challenges in reading and understanding.

Early in my career as a seminary teacher, I noticed that some students seemed to meet the challenge of the scriptures better than others. From class surveys, I learned that students who seemed to have a feel for the scriptures lived in families that had read the scriptures together as long as the students could remember. From what I knew about language development, I understood how a scripture-rich environment could have a significant impact.

Language Development Begins at Birth

From the first time an infant hears your voice, its active mind begins reaching out for language. My infant grandson, Nathan, turned and smiled when he heard his mother's voice. He was not so sure about Grandpa's voice, but soon he was smiling at that sound, too. He quickly learned that certain sounds of language relate to a family that loves him. Nathan actively listened as he learned the meaning of different language sounds. Soon he moved from a general to a more specific awareness of language and how it related to his immediate needs. My year-old granddaughter is now very much aware of the relationship of language to food, having diapers changed, cuddling, and other basic needs. It is a remarkable thing to watch your children as they begin to respond to language.

The first patterns recognized by infants are rhythm and intonation. Some refer to these as the melody of language. Children quickly understand that some sounds are associated with love and security while others may invoke feelings of tension and disapproval. Later, an awareness of specific sound patterns and words develops as children relate a few words and phrases to experiences in their lives. Early in this process they begin to understand how language works. This results in an intuitive sense that enables them to understand and respond. During these experiences children actively learn new language skills that help them respond to their environment.

The Special Language of the Scriptures

But what has this to do with scripture learning? What is true of language development in general has a special application for the unique language of the scriptures. My grandchildren learn about regular language naturally because it surrounds them. In contrast, we don't speak the language of the scriptures, which in some ways makes the scriptures like a second language. The only time children hear the language of the scriptures is when they are read aloud. As my daughter reads the scriptures to her baby, she is introducing the unique sounds and forms of scriptural language. As my granddaughter hears the scriptures read aloud, her understanding of that type of language is reinforced.

First Reading Experiences

It is never too early to begin reading the scriptures with your children. Right now, my granddaughter Hailey, three months old, does not seem to pay much attention to my reading efforts. She is content to passively listen while looking around the room. From my prior experience with my own children, I know that she will soon begin to watch my face as I read. She will carefully observe my changing expressions and attend more specifically to my reading.

While Hailey represents the beginning of this stage, my granddaughter Camille, age two, is at the end. She not only listens to the reading but is also interested in the pictures I show her while reading. She enjoys scripture picture books and has a few favorite stories that she likes read again and again. This is appropriate as repetition builds the familiarity important at this age. As I read to her, I watch carefully to see if she is interested. I usually cut my reading short rather than read beyond her interest level. At times she is very interested; at other times she has less interest. I think it is best to be sensitive to her readiness to participate and be careful not to overdo scripture reading. It is a joy when Camille sits on Grandpa's lap, happy to listen to scripture stories.

As Hailey grows, she too will be able to listen to a wider variety of stories and physically interact with books by reaching to touch the pages. Like Camille, she will begin to recognize familiar pictures and stories as her learning skills develop. When this happens I can begin to talk with her about the pictures. I will ask questions like, "What is that?" as I point to a colorful picture on the page. There may not be much of a response at first, but soon she will be able to respond with pre-language sounds. While Hailey will soon enjoy scripture storybooks, reading the actual scriptures will remain important as she continues to build her understanding of their unique language.

It is easy to underestimate the lasting influence of early

experiences with the scriptures. I am grateful that my children enjoyed the experience of being cuddled while hearing the scriptures read aloud again and again. Scripture attitudes and understandings are significantly affected by this simple effort.

Lap-Time Reading Ideas

As you consider these ideas, remember that the read-aloud activities should be modified to keep pace with your child's development. The following ideas will give you some alternatives to help you complement the basic reading experience.

Infants can "talk" about what is being read. Susan used this idea when reading to her son, Jeff, when he was a year old. To help him focus on the reading, she asked him questions and pointed out pictures when using a storybook. She found that he gave more attention to the reading when she also talked to him about what she was reading. While he didn't always understand, the talking seemed to focus the experience for him.

Don't hesitate to talk with your child during reading time and reinforce the idea that scriptures encourage people to talk about stories and ideas. These initial discussions may seem one-sided, but they will encourage language development. It is natural to use expressive language when talking with a child, and to overemphasize facial expressions. However, it is important to avoid baby talk because an example of normal speech better promotes language development.

Playthings can reinforce scripture learning. One of the scripture playthings our children enjoyed was a Noah's ark with stuffed animals that fit in pockets on the side. Stephen loved chewing on the animals before he learned that they fit in the pockets. When he discovered this, he loved pulling them out of the pockets after I tucked them inside. He would giggle as he found each animal and showed it to me. This toy was fun for Stephen, but it also reinforced his later understanding of the scripture story.

Young children explore their world through all their senses. That is why it is important to provide playthings for them to touch, hold, and examine. It is during this time that such items as a quiet book, soft toys, and bedroom mobiles on scripture themes can be introduced.

My friend made a scripture quiet book for her children. Using a regular quiet book as a model, she modified it so that her children could lace up Nephi's sandals, unbutton King Mosiah's robe, and pull Moroni's sword from his scabbard. She said it was not difficult to modify the existing pattern, and she felt confident that it helped her teach her child about people in the Book of Mormon.

Recently I saw a small photo album filled with scripture-related pictures that a mother had made for church. She had cut pictures from Church magazines and other sources and placed them in the album. She changed some of the pictures each month to maintain the child's interest. The pictures usually related to the family's scripture reading. It worked great except that their two-year-old often wanted to whisper the stories to her mom or dad during sacrament meeting. That was a good sign because it demonstrated the child's interest and involvement.

I have also seen a baby's room decorated with pictures or hanging mobiles based on scripture themes. In one room

I saw a picture of Jesus with a group of children. The mobile I liked best featured Book of Mormon characters made of bright, colored paper. It hung over the baby's crib and seemed to dance in the air.

During their childhood our boys had a picture of Helaman and his stripling warriors in their room. It came from a family home evening lesson on these great Book of Mormon heroes. The point of the lesson was that they would someday be called to serve like the sons of Helaman. I think that this small thing contributed to their desire to serve a mission.

Music complements the scriptures. One of our first family investments was a tape player. My wife knew that music was important, so she purchased a variety of tapes, some of which contained Primary songs. Listening to the recordings, I realized how many gospel truths were taught in these simple songs. Our children have grown up listening to Church music. I believe that as they listened to such music, they felt a special spirit. This enhanced their response to gospel truth, which reinforced a deeper appreciation for the scriptures.

While home teaching, I noticed that a family had a collection of Primary songs on compact discs. They explained that they played them in the morning before church started. They felt it created a Sabbath feeling in the home and helped prepare the family for their meetings later in the day. I was surprised at how well their children knew the Primary songs. It was a delight to hear them sing their favorites as the two-year-old stood on the sofa and led the rest of the children.

Children can have their own scriptures. Our children all

received their own scriptures before they could walk. I remember my son's first Book of Mormon. When he was old enough to hold the book, he immediately placed it in his mouth. I suppose this was his way of feasting on the scriptures. That book remained important to him for years and is now one of our family treasures.

Our children's copies of the Book of Mormon always had their names printed on the cover. That made the books personal and reinforced the importance of what we read.

One mother purchased an inexpensive Book of Mormon and then drilled a hole in a corner of the book through which she threaded fuzzy pink yarn. Her son, Mark, used this as a strap to carry the book around. In time Mark's Book of Mormon became as important to him as his favorite blanket.

Scripture learning is enhanced by storybooks. Storybooks should have colorful and interesting pictures that portray significant events. As you read the books aloud, your children can look at the pictures, which reinforce awareness and understanding. The pictures are often as important as the text. You should vary your reading by talking with your children about the pictures and allowing them to point at and touch the pictures. You may read from the actual scriptures while your children look at the pictures, or from the picture book itself.

The story session should be short. It is better to have several short stories than one longer one. Your children should experience a variety of books, but it is also important to continue reading from the scriptures themselves. Hearing the language of the scriptures is most important during the lap-time stage. By reading the scriptures you reinforce their unique rhythm, grammar, and vocabulary.

Family home evening ideas. My wife and I began holding family home evenings before our children were born. When our children did arrive, it was natural to involve them in our lessons. We thought it was wonderful to have them join us because they made us feel more like a family.

My friend described a family home evening with their eighteen-month-old child. They began by singing a Primary song and then showing the child pictures related to the lesson. They made a sign that read "Jesus loves Johnny" and hung it in the child's bedroom. He said that in this brief lesson they had felt the Spirit and knew that a wonderful thing had happened.

Another young mother involved her small children in art projects as they listened to the scriptures being read. The art projects helped them pay attention longer. She also cut pictures from the Church magazines she used in the lesson, and she placed the pictures on the cupboard as a reminder for her children. She recommended that every family purchase the Gospel Art Packet available from Church distribution. She found that these pictures were a valuable resource. Like these families, we found that our earliest home evenings were some of our best efforts.

Summary

It is never too early to introduce your children to the scriptures. It begins with the natural activity of holding them in your arms and reading aloud, which you should do regularly. The wonderful thing about scripture learning is that it is a natural outgrowth of a loving relationship with your child. The Spirit of the word of God combined with your love and testimony bless your small children more than you know. As they grow, you can introduce other experiences that complement this basic activity. Remember that during this stage it is important to develop an awareness of scriptural language. While music, quiet books, and pictures are important, it is the language of the scriptures that you want your children to experience. From this they will gain the awareness necessary for further development.

Activities for Children Ages Birth to Two

Activity	Purpose
1. Reading aloud. Read from the scriptures while cuddling or feeding your infant.	Develops an awareness of scriptural language.
2. Book talk. Talk to the infant while reading the scriptures.	Develops an awareness that discussion is an important part of learning about the scriptures.
3. Scripture quiet books. Create quiet books using scripture themes.	Develops familiarity with scripture characters and events.
4. Soft toys. Obtain soft toys that relate to the scriptures, such as Noah, his ark, and the animals.	Helps children learn about the scriptures through play.
5. Picture albums. Collect pictures from Church magazines.	Exposes children to a variety of scripture stories.
6. Room decorations. Hang pictures, mobiles, or other decorations related to the scriptures in your children's rooms.	Provides an environment that stimulates scripture awareness.
7. Music. Play music related to gospel themes, such as Primary songs.	Reinforces the spirit of the gospel, which enhances scripture learning.
8. Personal scriptures. Provide children with their own copies of the Book of Mormon.	Gives a sense of ownership and personal importance. Teaches that scriptures should be used and loved.
9. Picture storybooks. Purchase simple picture books that tell scripture stories with colorful and interesting pictures.	Interests children in scriptural images and stories.
10. Family home evening. Hold regular home evenings with pictures or art projects for children.	Helps children enjoy learning about the scriptures.

CHAPTER 4

Story Time

Three to Five: First Scripture Adventures

Children love a good story and often ask for it to be read again and again. The scriptures contain many stories that teach important truths. Read with a little imagination, these stories come alive in the minds of your children and help them feel the Spirit testifying of truth.

Our basement is filled with treasures from the past. Recently, while reorganizing this material to make room for a new generation of memories, I discovered a box from my childhood. Among the items it contained was an old cap pistol, a musty coonskin hat, and several books with faded red covers. The books were what remained of an old set of illustrated Bible stories that my mother read to me. I opened the books and found myself again hearing my mother's voice reading these wonderful stories. As I turned the pages, I recognized with fondness the familiar pictures and stories so important to me as a child. I am afraid my

efforts to reorganize the basement that morning took second place to reminiscing with my first scripture storybook.

Every child loves to listen to a good story and imagine
new worlds filled with wonderful things. Through stories
children see Abraham struggle to obey the Lord, walk with
Nephi through the dark streets of Jerusalem, and rejoice as
the sick and afflicted feel the touch of the Master's hand.
Stories from the scriptures teach children lessons from the
lives of faithful people who loved the Lord and relied on his
strength. Through these stories, testimonies grow as children identify with the great people whose lives inspire faith.

Children from ages three to five enjoy listening to scripture stories read aloud. Illustrated storybooks help them visualize important characters and events from the scriptures.

Children and Stories

Kayla looks forward to story time. Her mother knows
how much she enjoys her scripture storybooks and takes
advantage of her natural curiosity to encourage questions
while reading.

"Why didn't Nephi go to jail?" she asked while listening
to the story of how Nephi obtained the brass plates. When
her mother began to answer, Kayla noticed a bird outside
our window and forgot her question about Nephi.

When reading to younger children, their questions may
be more important than your answers because the questions
show that they are thinking. Often their energy won't allow
time for the answer you would like to give. But with
patience you will realize how much they are learning from
the stories you read together.

Later Kayla's mother asked her if she had thought about

why Nephi didn't go to jail. "He did what Heavenly Father asked him to," she replied, looking surprised that anybody would not know the answer to that question. Reading and talking with four-year-olds is always fun.

Mattie is five and can read some words by herself. She has favorite scripture stories that she wants read again and again. She can tell most of the stories in her own words, but she still likes to listen to her mom read them aloud. Mattie's increasing attention span enables her to enjoy repeated readings of a single story. She is becoming aware that some stories are true and others are fantasy, but frequently she has difficulty in separating fact from fiction when relating her favorite stories. Her comprehension of scripture stories often demonstrates unique and creative interpretations—maybe even unusual insights. Her mom encourages this because she knows that Mattie is trying to expand her understanding.

Reading Aloud to Children

During the first stage, reading aloud to children introduced the language of the scriptures. During the second stage, storybooks and picture books complement reading from the scriptures. Reading aloud from storybooks helps children understand the exciting stories found in the scriptures and identify with scriptural characters and events. Don't forget, however, that reading the actual language of the scriptures is still important. Storybooks simply balance and enhance the experience of reading directly from the scriptures.

Helps for Reading

You don't need special skills or materials to help your children love scripture stories. It will come as a natural result of reading and talking with your child. Remember, simple things work the best.

While there is no shortage of storybooks and picture books, they may vary in quality. Even though selecting a suitable book is personal, these guidelines may help. First, look carefully at the artwork. Younger children prefer simple, colorful pictures that highlight people. As they grow, they enjoy more complex pictures that illustrate the important events of the story. The artwork should be tasteful and not extreme. It should reflect the spirit of the scriptures in a colorful, interesting way. Good picture books have illustrations that children want to look at again and again.

Next consider the text of the story. Books are written at different reading levels. Avoid stories written in a mechanical style with simple "controlled vocabulary" for reading aloud. This type of book is useful in the next stage of development when children are becoming independent in their reading. But for this stage, the text should be interesting and exciting, and it should attract your children's attention.

The story should follow the scriptural account and convey the spirit the Lord intended. While fantasy is important to children's development, it is best left to books about nonscriptural topics. Scripture storybooks and picture books can be interesting without creating false images in children's minds. Remember, you are the best person to judge the quality of any book you are considering for your children. Choose carefully—they deserve the best.

Book Talk

We mentioned before the importance of talking with children while reading. Melissa is four and a half years old.

While her mom was reading the story of Adam and Eve, Melissa asked if there were any children in the garden of Eden. This presented Melissa's mother with a golden opportunity to teach important truths.

After the age of three, book talk grows in importance as oral language develops, enabling children to express their ideas. Much of this talk will be natural responses to your children's questions, but there are ways to direct and encourage discussion that develops different types of understanding.

As you consider the ideas below, do not anticipate doing all of them all the time. The basic activity is reading aloud and enjoying scripture stories with your children. Questions and related discussion should be natural; forced book talk is a distraction. In listening to your children's questions, be accepting and avoid being judgmental; each question is important to them. Also, be selective in using these ideas. You know best how to help your own children.

Have a plan. Think about what you can do or say before reading a particular story, while you are reading, and after you have finished reading. Encourage discussion that relates the story to something your children remember. For example, you might say, "Remember last time we read about Nephi breaking his bow? Today we will read how the family got their food without the bow and arrow." Another approach is to relate the story to an event in your children's lives. Randy described an experience with his five-year-old son. Before reading about the challenges Joseph faced before becoming a leader in Egypt, he said to his son, "This story reminds me of your brother in the mission field and how he depends on the Lord to help him." As Randy read about

Joseph, his son kept asking questions about his brother's mission. Randy was pleased that his son was able to see the relationship between the challenges faced by his missionary brother and those faced by Joseph in the Old Testament.

While reading, take a moment to talk about what the characters in the book are doing or what challenge they face. Then ask your children how they might be like the people in the story. While reading the story of Jonah, Joyce told her daughter that the prophet was afraid and did not want to do what the Lord commanded. She asked her daughter, "Have you ever been afraid of doing what was right?" What followed was an important discussion about her daughter's fear of giving her first talk in Primary. Joyce was reassured when her daughter said she would not be like Jonah and would not be afraid to give her talk. That day Joyce helped her daughter see the relevance of the scriptures to her own life.

After reading, help your children remember important facts and ideas from the story. Then encourage them to think about what they mean or how they apply in life. Jon ended a reading session by describing how brave Ammon was in defending the king's sheep. He then commented on how brave the missionaries are today. Another time, Jon asked his son to think of ways that he was like Nephi. The five-year-old responded that he always wanted to do what was right. Such exchanges are important in helping children understand the relevance of scripture stories.

During a shopping trip with my granddaughter, she noticed a large tree. She excitedly told me that it was just like the one in Lehi's dream. "But it doesn't have any fruit," she concluded. Such observations reflect children's attempts to relate the scriptures to things in their own lives. It is often the little things that make the difference.

Use pictures to encourage discussion. Pictures add meaning to scripture stories. Children often remember story events from the things they see in pictures. At first children will describe the people and things in the picture. Later they will begin to see the events represented by the pictures. "I see Nephi and his brothers" becomes "Nephi's brothers are angry with him."

Encourage looking at a story from a different perspective. While reading the account of Jesus teaching a lakeside sermon, Susan explained to her four-year-old daughter that the crowd was pushing Jesus backward toward the lake. Susan stopped reading and asked her daughter, "What should Jesus do? If he does nothing, he will soon be standing in the water!" "Oh, no!" said the daughter. "He needs a boat!" Susan then read with delight how Jesus borrowed a fishing boat and taught the people from the boat. Susan's daughter said with a sigh, "I'm glad he's safe." This type of situation provides an opportunity for you to encourage your children to find solutions or ideas that help solve problems suggested in the scriptures.

Older children in this stage may be ready for inferential questions. This type of question requires children to think about ideas that are suggested by the story but not stated directly. Typically such questions ask "why" or require a "because" kind of response. Connie asked her son, "Why did the people stop building the tower of Babel?" Her son answered, "They were really tired!" Connie then had the chance to explain more about the story.

Children may not always answer questions quickly, so be

patient and give them time to think. Their answers will usually be interesting and invite further discussion.

Once during family home evening, I showed our children a picture of Mormon and Moroni looking out over the battlefield. I asked them why Mormon looked so tired. "He must be a daddy!" my youngest son said. Such answers make reading the scriptures interesting and relevant to our lives.

You can also use questions that help children think about comparisons or contrasts. While showing a picture of Moses leading Israel across the Red Sea, one father asked his five-year-old, "How are the children of Israel different from the Egyptians chasing them?" Another example of this type of questioning is seen in a mother's question to her five-year-old: "As you look at this picture of Abinadi and wicked King Noah, who do you think is more powerful, the prophet or the wicked King?" Given the same picture, a question for younger children might be "Why is the King frowning and Abinadi not frowning?" As you help your child learn to look for such things, they develop the ability to consider what they know from their own experience and what the picture or text is telling them. This kind of thinking increases understanding.

Have children retell stories in their own words. Molly asked her Primary class to tell the story of Noah and the ark. One child told a creative version that included air-conditioning. He explained that without it the animals would have been "too hot." The creative adaptations in a child's retellings are always entertaining and important to their growing understanding of the scriptures.

Pictures can help children with their retellings. I watched a Primary teacher help a child remember the details of a story by looking at a picture. Holding a picture of Abraham and his son Isaac for the child to see, she asked her to tell the story. The child told how Isaac was to be sacrificed and how afraid he was. The teacher encouraged another look at the picture to help the child continue with the story. The picture kept her focused on the events as she remembered them.

Be careful when correcting your child's retellings. Focus only on the most important details; the process matters more than the product. One benefit of listening to retellings is that you will be able to sense if your children have understood the main idea of the story. While retellings need not be exact, as mentioned above, they should reflect a basic understanding of the scripture account and its teachings.

Point out key words. As children approach the end of this stage (age five) they may be able to remember and recognize certain printed words. To help my daughter with this, I wrote words that she had picked from our reading on recipe cards and taped them on the refrigerator door. She remembered names the best. Nephi, Helaman, and Samuel were no problem, but she often confused Mormon and Moroni.

I used another simple strategy to help focus her attention on words. I would use my finger to follow the words as I read to help her follow the line of print. When she saw a word she wanted to remember, I would stop and repeat the word for her and then allow her to read it to me. We then decided if we wanted to make a word card so she could remember it. We would practice the words on the cards to help her remember. If you try this activity, be careful not to force it, as children develop awareness of words at their own pace.

35

Explain difficult words. As you read to your children, you will encounter difficult words they may not understand. In reading about David and Goliath, our friend Erin read the phrase "five smooth stones out of the brook." "What's a brook?" her son asked. She had not thought to explain this word until he asked. She increased his understanding by responding, "A brook is like the little stream that runs behind grandpa's house."

At first you may just read difficult words without comment, but as the child matures you can stop and explain them. Do this naturally by reading the word in its sentence before you explain what it means. Sometimes children can figure out the meaning of a word just by hearing it in context. Doing this makes difficult words seem less threatening. I enjoyed helping my children understand the word *wo*. When they saw it, they knew that the Lord was talking about real trouble. As my youngest son said, "*Wo* means you got to get to bed right now!" Helping children understand selected words builds their understanding and appreciation of the scriptures.

Use art activities. My daughter gives each of her children crayons and paper when they read together. The girls color and draw while they listen to their mother read from the scriptures or a scripture storybook. After reading, they talk about their pictures and explain what they have to do with what was read. They are eager to display their pictures on the family bulletin board.

Encourage your children to visualize your reading by drawing pictures of what they heard about. This will expand their understanding as they express their own ideas through drawing, painting, or other art activities. Display their artwork so that others can share the joy of their creation. Talking with your children about their pictures will further reinforce what they have learned.

Our creative neighbor, Rosanne, enjoys planning art projects for her children. During one visit I saw that she had her son and daughter make puppets out of paper bags. They represented wicked king Ahab and the prophet Elijah. She was preparing the children to tell the story using their puppets.

I have seen so many refrigerator doors that have become the family bulletin board where children share their latest creations. It has been interesting to see what ends up on this bulletin board as the children grow older. We started with favorite Bible pictures and drawings and end up with seminary report cards and mission calls.

Be careful with scripture videos. My three-year-old granddaughter loves to watch videos. Her interest is so keen that her mom has to carefully monitor how much she watches. My daughter says it is a temptation to allow the video to baby-sit her daughter when there are so many things to be done. Videos are so attractive to children that they require our careful attention.

Children need little encouragement to watch scripture videos. Most presentations are well done and entertain as well as a Saturday morning cartoon. But at this stage the video may be more of a distraction than an aid to learning. The personal contact and interaction from reading aloud together cannot be duplicated with a video. Another disadvantage is that videos do not contribute to children's awareness of the unique language of the scriptures. Videos do have a productive role in promoting scripture learning, but caution is advised. I have found it best to limit the use of videos during this stage and instead look for ways to build language awareness and story appreciation.

Summary

The story-time stage continues to emphasize reading aloud to build scripture language skills. In addition, picture books and storybooks are useful in building understanding of important characters and events. Together the scriptures and storybooks provide the variety and balance that foster understanding.

Book talk encourages conversations about the scriptures. This can take several forms, each having a different objective. Again, variety and balance are important as different methods are adapted to meet your children's needs and interests. Be careful to avoid judging your children's responses to questions and discussion. This should be a time free from the risk of correction.

Artwork encourages scripture learning, especially when it is valued and displayed for others to appreciate. Videos may distract from scripture learning during this stage. They tend to limit early language learning and cannot personalize the scripture experience as parents can.

Learning to love the scriptures is the result of many experiences. Like tender plants, children respond to light and nurturing care. It is counterproductive to force a plant to grow. The same is true of forcing children to grow in their understanding of the scriptures. Given the proper environment and conditions, this growth will occur naturally and miraculously. Natural experiences work best. Understanding your children is the key to selecting and

modifying experiences that will build a love for the scriptures. Involving children and valuing their responses is
most important. When children are encouraged in this
manner, they naturally grow to appreciate the scriptures.
After all, you are their role model, and as you share your
love of the scriptures, they will naturally trust and accept
your efforts.

Activities for Children Ages Three to Five

Activity	Purpose
1. Read aloud from the scriptures. Regularly read aloud from the scriptures.	Reinforces the unique language of the scriptures.
2. Read aloud from storybooks. Read aloud from scripture storybooks and picture books.	Develops familiarity with scripture stories.
3. Book talk. Encourage discussion while reading. Ways to encourage discussion:	Encourages children to think about what is being read. Promotes understanding and memory of scripture stories.

a. *Relate stories to life.* Ask questions before, during, and after reading to help children apply the scriptures.

b. *Encourage children to make predictions.* Ask what they think will happen next in the story.

c. *Ask "because" and "why" questions.* Ask questions that require children to think of reasons or explanations.

d. *Compare and contrast.* Encourage children to look for differences and similarities between characters or events.

e. *Have children retell stories.* Ask them to retell the main events of the story in their own words.

f. *Point out key words.* Point out key words for the child to remember. Start with character names.

g. *Explain words.* Stop and explain difficult words that the child may not understand.

Activity	Purpose
4. Artwork. Encourage art projects that help children express what they learn from the scriptures.	Helps children express what they have learned and reinforces understanding and appreciation. Also stimulates and maintains interest.
5. Videos. Limit exposure to videos.	Reading aloud to establish language skills is most important at this stage.

CHAPTER 5

Play Time

Six to Eleven: Having Fun With Scriptures

Learning requires an active mind and body. Children love to do as they learn. Listening and watching are not enough; children want to experience things for themselves. Combining play with scripture learning enhances children's appreciation for the word of God.

Our children often attended Primary twice a week. The first session was held at our local chapel under the direction of faithful teachers and leaders. The other session met in our basement playroom. Barbie, G.I. Joe, My Little Pony, and a variety of stuffed animals would sit quietly and listen to Primary lessons taught by our daughters. Through play they rehearsed and learned roles important to their developing testimonies.

All children play to learn. Their love of play provides an opportunity to include scripture activities as part of this experience. Through such activities, we enhance their understanding of the stories, characters, and principles found in the scriptures. Play activities create enthusiasm and energy for learning important truths. If we take children's play seriously, we will discover many ways to help them understand and love the scriptures.

Primary Children

After teaching our children about baptism, my wife and I were not surprised to see them acting out the ordinance in the backyard with their friends. Children between the ages of six and eleven learn best by playing. For six-year-olds, this is especially true. Their increased learning ability combines with enthusiasm and energy that easily tire most adults. As a result, learning proceeds best when six-year-olds are involved physically as well as mentally. Drawing pictures for use in family home evening was a favorite activity for our sons. They enjoyed illustrating stories from the scriptures used in our lessons. They would carefully listen to the lesson, eager for the time when they could display their artwork.

Ages seven to eight are characterized by increased independence. Individuality is growing, and children begin having their own ideas. Growing intellectual skills enable children to participate in problem-solving activities. Games become an important part of family scripture activities. My children enjoyed creating games that helped teach or review scripture principles. One of their favorites involved turning the family room into a miniature golf course. Each family member had to answer a scripture question before trying to putt a golf ball into a paper cup taped to the floor.

Important changes from ages seven to eight affect scripture learning. First, children develop a sense of accountability, accompanied by a growing acceptance of responsibility and a desire to do what is right. Second, they become less dependent on their parents as they establish their own identities. Finally, they prefer activities that challenge them to think in different ways and learn new things.

Children ages nine through eleven have a growing interest in peer relationships. They seek group association as dependence on their family begins to decrease. Feelings of loyalty and friendship increase in importance when they begin to associate with social groups outside the family. Group learning becomes productive because they are able to work with other children in learning new things. Our sons loved the Cub Scout program for this reason. As parents, we were grateful for Scouting's emphasis on service and duty to God. We appreciated the teachings and activities that paralleled our own efforts to encourage scripture learning.

With a longer attention span, children at this age enjoy extended learning experiences that are challenging and require more than just listening. They enjoy playing a variety of games that allow them to demonstrate what they have learned from the scriptures. I found it fun to put key scriptures on index cards. With the help of my children I wrote a scripture reference on one side of the card, and on the other we wrote three questions related to the scripture. These cards were then displayed on the refrigerator door during the week to remind the children of our discussions. We also used these cards for an activity patterned after the game of concentration. This game required us not only to understand the scripture but also to remember details about it.

During this stage boys and girls become increasingly different. The maturation of the girls accelerates, enabling

43

them to focus and learn more quickly. Girls find it easier to sit and listen, while boys require a more active approach. Boys begin to exhibit a sense of self that can cause moodiness and disinterest. In response to spiritual moments, girls may display their emotions more readily; boys are sometimes more hesitant. This is a time of change as both boys and girls prepare for the challenge of adolescence.

Reading aloud to your Primary-aged children remains an important part of a balanced approach to scripture learning. Their growing independence will enable them to begin reading on their own. While encouraging independence, you should also continue reading the scriptures aloud with your children to continue developing their familiarity with scriptural language. During the previous two stages, you cuddled your children on your lap while you read aloud from the scriptures. While lap time does not disappear at age six, it does begin to change as children mature and develop a wider range of interests. Family scripture time usually takes precedence over personal time for children six and older. However, having recognized this, wise parents will always look for opportunities to share the scriptures individually with each child.

Family Scripture Reading

Before reading as a family, parents need to decide whether the family should read a specific number of verses or for a given period of time. Most families read a selected number of verses each day. However, reading for a set time is an alternative worth considering, as it allows for discussion and questions. Because the emphasis is not on completing a definite number of verses, family members feel more free to discuss ideas or ask questions.

The goal is to make family scripture reading less mechanical. You should encourage your family to do more than just take turns reading and listening with little opportunity for discussion. To do this, consider ways to raise the quality of family scripture reading and yet remain practical. The following suggestions may help.

Talk about the scriptures. Talking with your children is as important as reading to them. We read about the things we talk about, and we talk about the things we read about. This cycle is important in promoting scripture reading and understanding.

To create a context for scripture discussions, ask a family member to provide a brief introduction to the scripture to be read. This prepares family members by alerting them to characters, events, and ideas in the passage. One example is our family's experience with David and Goliath. Before reading the passage, we explained to our children who the Philistines were and why they were fighting King Saul and the armies of Israel. We then displayed a life-size drawing of Goliath. It was fun for the children to measure the dimensions of Goliath on the wall. Doing these things ahead of time prepared our family to read the account with increased interest and understanding.

Set a purpose. Setting a purpose before reading establishes a definite reason for the activity. You can accomplish this by asking a question or suggesting that family members look for a particular bit of information. For example, before reading the account of Alma at the waters of Mormon, ask your family to look for something unusual about the first baptism performed by Alma. This will engage your family in an interesting discussion about baptism and Alma's unique experience.

One father described how his family encouraged discussion as part of their reading activity. In family home evening they would decide on a topic from the Topical Guide. Each day they would then locate and read several scriptures from the list. After reading the scriptures, they would summarize what they had learned about the topic from their reading. This is a productive way to promote scripture-based understanding of Church doctrine.

Ask questions. After providing background and directions to look for specific information, read several verses of scripture without interruption. After reading the block, stop and talk together about what was read. This brief discussion may be initiated by asking such questions as, "How do you think this answered the question we asked before reading?" or "What do you think will happen next when we read tomorrow?" This type of discussion helps families summarize and draw conclusions about their reading. The quality of the experience increases as discussion brings reading to life.

Encourage independence. As children reach age eleven, their increasing maturity enables them to participate more fully as readers as well as listeners. This is a time to encourage them to contribute to family scripture discussions. Let them lead the discussion and suggest questions that look past the surface meaning of the story to a deeper understanding. You may be surprised at how well they do. This is a time when reading and listening expand to include other language skills. Writing and talking become important as children learn to respond to new information in a variety of ways. As you encourage this new independence, your children's confidence will grow.

Build a home library. Because children's reading ability varies so much between six and eleven, it is important to provide them with a variety of books. My family's home library is now rather worn and tattered. Our collection of children's books shows the effects of many years and many small hands. We believed that books, lots of them, belonged in our home. It was no surprise that Christmas and birthdays always involved books as gifts. There were so many good books for children to read that it was always a delight to go shopping. It was no problem to select one or two books for each child. As the children grew, our libraries grew, and soon our shelves were filled with a wide variety of books. Now our grandchildren benefit as we help their personal libraries grow.

A home library that contains many different kinds of books encourages reading. The more children read, the more skilled they become at reading, which in turn enables them to read even more. My earliest memories of books my mother read to me are *Puff and Toot* and Bible storybooks. While my interest in *Puff and Toot* passed, my reading in the Bible storybooks provided a foundation for a continued interest in the scriptures.

Each child's bedroom should have a shelf to hold their favorite books. Some of the books can be from the home library. Others can be part of the child's own collection, received as gifts or purchased with money earned from household chores. Even though most of the child's collection will not be related to the scriptures, there will be those favorites that the child will treasure and enjoy reading again and again.

One advantage of the bedroom bookshelf is that it comes in handy when children are ready for bed. For our own sanity, we discovered it was best to have a regular bedtime for our children. There were many nights when they were not tired and wanted to stay up. Our stock phrase was, "I'm sorry, it's bedtime. But you may read for ten minutes before we turn out the lights." Because of the interesting books in the children's rooms, this was usually fine with them.

Scripture books are an important part of a home collection. Bible stories need not dominate the shelf but should be part of a home library. Early in our experience we purchased a set of Book of Mormon picture books that proved most useful over the years as we read and re-read these stories. Later we purchased the Church history and Bible sets to complement our Book of Mormon collection. While these seemed expensive at the time, we found them to be a good investment over the years. In addition to the scripture-oriented book sets, we found that local bookstores offered a wide variety of children's books that focus on scripture topics. Over time we built a collection of books that told stories from both ancient and modern scripture. When these books are part of a balanced home collection, your children will frequently select and read them. This reinforces your effort to encourage scripture understanding and appreciation.

Use public libraries. Most public libraries contain Bible storybooks. As part of a general plan to teach your children the value of libraries, help them locate and check out scripture books. The limitation of a library book is that it is not always available when your child would like to read it. That is one reason why we determined to have our own family library as a permanent resource.

Selecting Books for Primary Children

Earlier we noted that books for younger children should contain simple but interesting stories and colorful illustrations. We recommended that "controlled vocabulary" books were not appropriate for children under six. However, as your children's reading skills mature, you will need to modify the criteria for selecting books.

Select storybooks that help your child read. In deciding which books to buy, remember to look for books that encourage the growing independence of your children. More and more they will want to read on their own as well as with you. That is why you will want to consider purchasing "controlled vocabulary" books that contain scripture stories written with a basic vocabulary. This type of book is usually not as interesting to read; the language is mechanical and artificial because of limited word choice. However, this disadvantage is offset by the independence this offers beginning readers. The basic vocabulary helps children read with confidence as their new skills develop.

You may need patience to listen to your children read from a controlled vocabulary book, but it is worth the effort to hear them say, "I can read it myself." It is fun to listen when they carefully read each word, frequently stopping to look for your approval. The books best suited for this usually have a small amount of print and many colorful and interesting pictures. The best books have pictures that help your children understand more fully what they are reading.

As your children's reading skills develop, you should select books that match their increasing reading level. One way to test the appropriateness of the book is to have your children read a page aloud to you. If they make more than five mistakes, the book is probably too difficult. This is called the "five-finger rule." It is commonly used by reading teachers and librarians. As you listen to your children read, you will soon develop a feel for their reading level.

Don't hesitate to help your children with words they don't recognize. A good way to do this with a beginning reader is to read with them. This technique is sometimes called "echo" or "shadow" reading because the child repeats the words you read from the passage. Have your child sit next to you, and as you read aloud, follow the words with your finger. Encourage your child to repeat what you say and follow your finger on the page. After the first few times your child will be able to echo your reading. This is a proven technique often used in schools to promote reading development.

As your children mature they will be able to read a wider variety of books and more of the scriptures, too. The scriptures may remain a challenge, but with your help, your children will be able to read with surprising comprehension. Reading a combination of religious storybooks and the scriptures themselves is important in developing self-sufficiency in scripture reading.

Look for pictures that teach. The pictures and illustrations in books usually serve one of three purposes. First, they can be used to decorate the book, making it attractive to the reader. Second, they may illustrate characters and events from the story in an attempt to help the reader understand. Finally, pictures can be designed to invite the reader to interact with the story and think about key ideas.

Decorative pictures, while attractive and appealing, do little to help children understand the story. Most children's books avoid such pictures.

More commonly, pictures in children's books are illustrative or representative. Such pictures help readers understand by depicting what is happening. They may be simple character representations or complex portrayals of events from the story. In selecting a book, be sure to inspect the illustrations to see how well they relate to the story.

The third type of picture, interactive, is becoming more common in children's books, especially those for older children. Interactive pictures teach new material and invite readers to think more carefully about the information in the text. For example, an interactive picture might show a detailed drawing of Herod's temple, where Jesus taught. The scriptures themselves do not give enough information for readers to visualize the place, but an interactive illustration could. A growing number of Bible storybooks now use this type of illustration. Maps and charts can also be interactive because they require readers to interpret the information and apply it to the story. For example, a map showing the distance between Nazareth and Bethlehem would help children better understand the Christmas story.

Scripture Activities for Primary Children

Family traditions are important, and the scriptures can be part of those traditions. Our family decided that the scriptures would play a central part in our Christmas, Easter, and other holiday traditions. For example, one of our traditions is to celebrate April 6 with a sunrise service. The week before that day, our children prepare talks from the scriptures. Their talks might be about Easter, the Savior's birth, or the First Vision. (You'll recognize that all of these are spring events that occurred on or near April 6.) As the day draws near, I check the newspaper for the time of sunrise and then locate just the right spot to watch it. On the big day we bundle up and drive to the location before the sun comes up. We sing songs and share what we have prepared from the scriptures. The event concludes with a family picture and breakfast in a local restaurant.

This is a great, scripture-centered tradition that our family has enjoyed for many years. But such activities have little effect if parents do not set the example by regularly studying the scriptures themselves. Children who see their parents reading the scriptures have an advantage because they know how important the scriptures are to those they love the most. Keep this in mind as you read the following ideas for scripture activities. They are based on the assumption that the children have parents who consistently show their love for the scriptures.

So many activities are possible that it would be impossible to list them all. What follows is a representative selection of some of the more useful ones. Remember that the purpose of these activities is to encourage scripture learning and involve children in discovering new ideas from the scriptures.

Art Activities

My wife maintained a family art center that contained paper of different kinds, crayons, markers, scissors, glue, and other art materials. You can use such tools in a variety of activities that encouraging scripture learning.

Coloring books are available at local bookstores and allow children to color their favorite Bible or Book of Mormon characters and scenes. Younger children enjoy coloring pictures related to family scripture reading.

Cut-outs are fun for children. Past issues of Church magazines are an excellent source of pictures related to the scriptures. When these are cut out and mounted on heavy paper, they can be used to illustrate scripture reading.

Puppets can be easily made of old socks or cut-out figures mounted on sticks. There is no shortage of ideas for puppets in children's magazines. The purpose of these is to help children tell scripture stories through puppet dramas. My children loved to kneel behind the sofa and hold their homemade puppets so that all could see their scripture play. They not only learned from this activity, but they also provided instruction that entertained the family. One of our favorite activities involved making characters out of play dough. The children would identify important characters from a scripture passage and mold them from clay. Then the children would move the characters around the kitchen table as they reenacted the story. The boys enjoyed dramatizing Captain Moroni stories from the book of Alma and often created weapons from toothpicks to make their stories more realistic.

Story drawings can be made on a large sheet of poster or butcher paper. Children may create a mural or place pictures in boxes as in a newspaper cartoon. These works of art can be very detailed, as the children study the scriptures and listen to what was read in order to know what to draw. My family displayed the drawings in our home and enjoyed watching the children repeatedly stop and look intently at their own drawings. A good follow-up activity is to have the children use their story drawings to retell the stories they have illustrated.

Craft Activities

Simple art projects can be expanded into more extensive undertakings. Older children are more successful with these activities because some skill is required.

Storybooks can be made from simple materials. Cardboard covers and typing paper can be tied together with yarn to create a simple book. Children can decorate the cover with a picture and title. Then they can write the scripture story in their own words on the pages inside. I made my daughter's first storybook by having her tell me the scripture story while I wrote her words in her book. She then illustrated each page with a drawing that represented something from the story. Through the years I collected a library of original storybooks, providing many memories related to my children's growing understanding of the scriptures.

Scripture collages are fun for older children. Magazines and newspapers are a good source of scripture-related pictures. If the topic is "the riches of the world," children can search for pictures related to it. Then they can paste the pictures on posterboard to make a collage. Such a display reinforces the scripture lesson and helps children relate to the message.

Scripture journals allow children to write a response to what they have heard read or are reading independently. These are not retellings of the story but personal reflections on what the story means to them. We found that keeping a family scripture journal was a good way to create interest in family scripture reading. To involve all our family in this activity, our younger children would share their thoughts while an older child or parent recorded the ideas in the family scripture journal. The children enhanced the simple written entries with elaborate illustrations. We enjoyed sharing our thoughts with the rest of the family. Some great lessons and insights are written in the pages of our scripture journal.

When our family purchased our first computer, it became a favorite way for the children to keep their journals. Even our youngest daughter was involved. She liked telling her thoughts to others and then watching her words appear on the screen as we typed them for her. When it was her turn, we could always count on her to provide a colorful illustration with her entry. I have found that home computers are great tools for creating a family journal.

Scripture scrapbooks can also be an individual or family project. They are made from pictures and artwork organized to reflect family scripture reading. As a family project, each person takes a turn creating a page for the scrapbook. The page must contain pictures or personal artwork that relate to family scripture study or personal scripture study. The children enjoy the activity and often demonstrate unique scripture insights.

Scripture Drama

For almost thirty years, my family has enjoyed an annual family Christmas pageant. We have a rule that the children must participate in the pageant until they find someone to replace them. Our oldest daughter now has three replacements, and our next daughter will soon have two of her own. The other children are good sports, and together with the grandchildren, the pageant continues. Angels with flashlights herald the birth of the Christ child, and shepherds with towels on their heads visit Mary and Joseph. The annual drama concludes with Grandpa reading the Christmas story. This is only one way to use drama to reinforce scripture learning; others are described below.

Slide shows provide a great way to encourage dramatic retellings of scripture accounts. The participants dress in costumes suitable for the story; scenes are staged, and pictures are taken. A slide show is then created, and the children add a narration to complete their dramatic interpretation of the scripture account.

Video shows have some advantages over slide shows. In a video production you can add sound and action. The scripts can be planned or spontaneous. We prefer the latter and have found that insight comes as children use their own words instead of those in the scriptures. In making a video, one family member becomes the director to help move the production to completion. What fun it is to hear the director shout "Cut!" to stop the camera and explain why Nephi should show more feeling as he decides what to do about Laban. Scripture learning is enhanced by such activities.

Mini-dramas are usually spontaneous activities that involve family members in a short dramatic reenactment related to a scripture passage. Roles are assigned and the scenes explained before the actors respond. The activity should be limited to a single scripture scene that involves only a few characters. The mini-drama lasts only long enough to illustrate an idea that is part of a larger lesson or reading assignment.

Silent dramas are mini-dramas in which the participants are not allowed to speak. Participants must convey thoughts and ideas with actions rather than words. While this can be frustrating, it is entertaining and causes the participants to think carefully about what is happening in the scriptures.

Reading Activities

During family reading time, it is important to vary the things you do as you read. Reading mechanically has little influence on children. If you add variety, family scripture reading will be much more interesting.

Objects can be used to introduce a scripture passage. Placing a stone on the table before reading the story of Stephen in the book of Acts will help your children better understand the bravery of that man. I found an old railroad spike, the kind used to hold rails to the wooden ties. I saved it until our Easter family home evening. At that time I had each person hold the heavy spike while I explained how such a spike was driven into the hands and feet of Christ. The object brought a reality to our reading of the scriptures that described the final days of Christ's life, and it gave us a greater appreciation of this sacred moment.

Questions are important when reading with older children. Questions asked before reading help establish a purpose for reading. Questions asked during the reading draw attention to key ideas in the passage. Questions asked after the reading help children apply the scriptures to their own lives. As your children grow older, ask them to read aloud the passage that answers the question; then have them explain why they picked that particular scripture. Asking questions may limit the amount you can read each day, but it will increase your children's understanding of the scriptures. We've found a helpful variation of this activity. After a family member reads, he or she asks a question for the rest of us to answer. Sometimes the questions are most insightful. For example, after reading about Nephi's breaking his bow, my young son asked if Nephi said he was sorry. I had to think about that question.

Signal word switch is another way to bring variety to your family scripture reading. Before reading, select several signal words. Usually these are connector words, such as *in, on,* and *therefore*. As family members read aloud, they watch for the signal words. When someone reaches the first signal word, he or she stops reading, and the next person immediately begins reading aloud until reaching the second signal word. Family members must pay careful attention not to miss the signals that indicate a change in the reader.

Strips in a jar provides an alternative to traditional family scripture reading. To prepare for this activity, write scripture references on slips of paper and place them in a jar. Next, ask family members to draw a slip of paper and read the reference written on it. After reading the scripture, the person must explain it in his or her own words. This activity is especially useful if the family goal is to read to better understand a topic, such as baptism or resurrection. Using this activity, a family can read a wide selection of scriptures on a given topic.

A Scripture-Rich Home

A scripture-rich home contains visible evidence of an active interest in the scriptures. This evidence can have a profound effect on children.

Family prayer is a time to pray about the things the family reads in the scriptures. It is natural to express gratitude for the scriptures and ask for further understanding. This reinforces the importance of the scriptures and blesses the family.

Stories from Church magazines can provide modern applications for scripture teachings. It can also help children broaden their understanding of how the scriptures can help with life's challenges.

A *picture of the month* is an activity that contributes to a scripture-rich home. Each month a picture is displayed in a visible place in the home. The refrigerator is a common place, but you may have a family bulletin board or other special place. The picture should relate to family scripture reading and provide a visible reminder of what is being read. Children can be involved in the effort to create a scripture-centered home by finding and preparing the picture of the month.

Word cards are used to reinforce key words from the scriptures. The children choose words from the scriptures that they think are important. They print these words on index cards, which are mounted on colored paper and displayed in the home. When the children notice the words, they are reminded of what was read. This activity also reinforces scripture vocabulary, which contributes to improved reading. It is important that your children choose the words, which will be those they personally think are worth remembering. They can also color, decorate, or personalize the words as desired, which will also help them remember.

Charts and graphs help some families develop the habit of reading the scriptures. Each member of the family is listed on a chart, and when each person reads a predetermined scripture selection, he or she receives recognition with a mark or a sticker. Many children love stickers, and the incentive to earn them encourages children to remember to read. The chart can be used to encourage both family and individual scripture reading. The more colorful the chart and the more interesting the stickers, the more likely it is that children will respond.

Commercial Materials

The variety of commercial materials is growing as members of the Church become interested in scripture-centered activities.

Scripture activity books provide a wide range of independent and family activities. There are two basic types of commercial activity books. The most common is the skill book. Skill books require children to complete such activities as solving a puzzle, following a maze, or completing a word activity. These activities are based on conventional reading development workbooks. They focus on visual discrimination, fine-motor coordination, alphabet learning, phonic awareness, and other skills related to general reading development. In an attempt to interest Church members, conventional activities are rewritten with scripture themes. These activities succeed at developing reading skills directly and scripture understanding indirectly.

The second type of commercial activity book directly enhances scripture understanding. One variety rewrites a story from the scriptures, leaving out key words. Sometimes the missing words are replaced with blanks, sometimes with pictures. The child is expected to read the story and fill in the missing words. Not only are reading skills enhanced, but the child also reviews an important scripture story. Another type of activity asks the child to look at a set of pictures that relate to a scripture event. The pictures are out of sequence. The child is expected to review the story and rearrange the pictures into their correct order. These activities develop scripture understanding. Frequently the *Friend* magazine uses activities of this type.

Scripture videos are growing in popularity. They are professionally prepared in a way that appeals to children. Earlier I cautioned about showing scripture videos to younger children. Videos lack the personal touch needed to build language skills and encourage a lifelong interest in the scriptures. But as children grow older, there is a place for videos. From six to eleven, children have a reasonable grasp of the unique language of the scriptures and are familiar with many stories. Because they have their own ideas about the scriptures, they are prepared to consider the interpretation presented by the video, which may enhance their understanding. On the other hand, if a child's first exposure to the scriptures is through videos, the images are so powerful that they will determine a child's interpretation for years to come.

Be careful with commercial videos. They can create the same trap that exists with television. Children's television does not typically require active participation or thinking. Television can rob your children of the experiences necessary in developing reading and language skills. Like children's television programs, scripture videos are best if watched with a parent who can place them in a context of family discussion and related scripture reading. If your family were to read the story of Lehi's dream and talk about it before watching the video version, the video could then enhance the discussion and increase learning. It is your involvement that is key to maximizing the effect of the video presentation.

Some parents find the video a convenient babysitter when no alternative exists. When this happens, there is a benefit in letting children watch scripture videos along with other commercial videos. You just need to be careful that you use scripture videos in a balanced family approach to the scriptures.

Summary

Primary-age children learn best through a variety of activities. Reading aloud remains important as your children continue to develop awareness of scripture language. Listening to your children read becomes important as they develop independence in their own reading.

Family scripture reading becomes more interesting when you encourage discussion. Activities that encourage your family to talk about what they are reading promote learning. As you invite your children to read and listen to a variety of books, it is helpful to have a home library that includes scripture picture books and storybooks.

Art and drama are useful in promoting scripture reading. They encourage children to express their scripture learning with their individual talents. Your home should reflect your interest in the scriptures. Pictures, display boards, and home libraries are helpful.

While activities enhance learning through variety, these can be limited if your children do not see you reading the scriptures. Your example is most important.

Activities for Children Ages Six to Eleven

Activity	Purpose
1. Reading aloud from the scriptures. Read aloud from the scriptures on a regular basis.	Reinforces the unique language of the scriptures.
2. Family scripture reading. Read and discuss gospel topics as a family.	Promotes scripture reading and understanding.
3. Selecting books. Careful attention to vocabulary and the type of illustration will help in the selection of appropriate books.	Choose books that encourage the growing independence of your children.
a. *Build a home library.* Collect children's books related to the scriptures.	
b. *Match books to reading level.* Controlled vocabulary, helpful pictures and illustrations, five-finger rule.	Children learning to read rely on simple vocabulary and pictures that help them understand what they read.
4. Scripture activities. Activities encourage scripture learning and involve children in discovering new things from the scriptures.	Children can express what they have learned through different activities.
a. *Artwork.* Coloring books, cut-out activities, puppets, story drawings.	Children can use different materials to create puppets, drawings, etc. to express their ideas.
b. *Craft activities.* Storybooks, collages, illustrated journals.	These activities expand the basic art activities into more extensive projects.
c. *Drama and media.* Mini-drama, silent drama, slide shows, video shows.	Children use their natural creativity to reinforce their understanding of the scriptures through planning and presenting a dramatic presentation.
d. *Reading.* Relating objects to ideas, asking different types of questions, strips in a jar.	Reading remains central to the development of scripture understanding. A variety of reading experiences encourages reading.
e. *Commercial materials.* Scripture activity books, scripture videos, Church magazines.	Commercial materials provide a variety of ways to interest children in learning more about the scriptures.

CHAPTER 6

Teaching Time

Twelve to Eighteen: Learning From the Scriptures

The teen years are a time of increasing independence and learning. Important decisions are made during these years about missions, education, and temple marriage. The scriptures are an essential part of this experience. Without their influence our youth can flounder and lose their way.

The years between twelve and eighteen are filled with many challenges. At times my wife and I wondered if our efforts had any effect in the lives of our teenagers. In their struggle for maturity, they did not always seem to understand or appreciate our encouragement. It required patience and preparation on our part to help them with the scriptures.

During one family home evening we had decided to teach our children about Lehi's dream. After we read the account in the Book of Mormon and showed pictures to promote understanding, it was time for an activity that

65

reinforced the main idea of the lesson. The younger children were excited and eager to participate. However, our teenager was ready for the closing prayer; she wanted to prepare for school the next day. After a little encouragement she put on her "I'm not really interested" face and waited for me to proceed.

The activity required the children to walk across a two-inch board placed between two blocks. I told them that this balance beam was the narrow path we had read about in Lehi's dream. They understood that if they fell off the beam, they would fall into the filthy river mentioned in the dream. They walked carefully and had no problem crossing the beam. Next I reminded them of the mists of darkness that clouded the narrow trail. I blindfolded each of the children and asked them to walk the beam again without the advantage of sight. Each one fell and after trying several times admitted that it was more difficult when they were blindfolded. I then asked the family members to reread selected verses to learn how to succeed when the mists of darkness come. Our teenager grudgingly participated in what she perceived as a childish activity.

The children identified the iron rod described in the dream, and we discussed its purpose. Again we asked the children to walk the beam blindfolded. I told them this time there would be an iron rod, if they felt for it. As the blindfolded children hesitantly began to walk the beam, they reached out to find the iron rod. When they did so, they grasped a broom handle my wife and I held beside them. Crossing the beam became easy when they held the handle. I explained that the iron rod was like the broom handle that keeps us balanced when the temptations of the devil cloud our vision. The lesson was a success, and we felt that our children understood. Of course, our teenager was the first to leave the family room, intent on other things in her busy life.

A week later she came home from school sad and disappointed. In a tender moment she related what had happened. We knew it was to have been her big day as she had been asked to join the school sports club. The club had asked her to meet in the gym after school for the initiation of the new members. The girls in the club had formed a circle and invited the nominees to stand in the middle of the circle one at a time. The club president then whispered to each potential member an embarrassing thing they had to do before the group as part of the initiation. Some were asked to crow loudly and walk like a chicken; others did silly dances or made funny faces, causing the club members to laugh at the embarrassment of the initiates. When it was our daughter's turn, the president whispered to her the embarrassing thing she was to do. Her assignment was to shout at the top of her voice a swear word. While this may have been perceived as a harmless expectation to most in the group, none of whom were members of the Church, to our daughter it presented a real dilemma.

If she shouted the word, all would laugh, and she would be accepted as a member of the club, but what would happen if she refused? She stood for what seemed to her like an eternity trying to decide what to do. Closing her eyes, she offered a quick prayer and then felt something in her hand. For the briefest moment she remembered holding the broom handle in family home evening. As the mists of darkness clouded her vision, she found an iron rod. Knowing what she had to do, she left the circle and walked out of the gym. Finding a place where she could be alone, she cried tears of disappointment before returning home.

We are grateful for the lesson from the scriptures that helped our teenage daughter make a difficult decision. The Lord does bless us for our faith, and while she did not join that sports club, she did continue her athletic career and played an important part on her high school championship basketball and track teams. We were grateful that the lesson of the iron rod blessed our daughter at an important time in her life.

Our youth are difficult at times and may not appear to find the scriptures as interesting as they did when they were younger. But at this critical time in their lives, they do need the blessings that come from the scriptures. We can meet the challenges of teaching our youth and provide instruction that blesses their lives.

Characteristics of Youth Learners

While youth between the ages of twelve and eighteen are complex, there are certain basic characteristics that most teenagers share. Their rapid physical growth seems to surprise us all. It seems that one day they are children and the next they have new adult bodies. This change often proves to be as awkward for the youth as it is for the parents.

Intellectually their ability to make objective judgments improves. They continue to prefer concrete learning experiences, but their skill at abstract reasoning is developing. They don't always accept things they are taught, and they often question the explanations of others. They develop their own ideas and opinions on a wide range of subjects and are eager to express them. However, in spite of their enthusiasm, they frequently have difficulty providing logical explanations for some of their conclusions.

Socially, youth are egocentric and feel that the entire world is looking at them. This makes them feel self-conscious, and self-criticism is common. This can lead to a loss of confidence expressed in defensive feelings, rebellion, or withdrawal. In this time of change and exploration, most youth feel that they are the first ones ever to experience life and that their experiences are unique. This false understanding can make it difficult for them to learn from their parents.

Youth find comfort with their peers while they struggle to gain independence from their parents. They find that their peers provide them with the confidence necessary to become independent from their parents. This can be both a positive and negative influence as our youth make important decisions.

The Challenge

Motivation is at the heart of encouraging youth to read and study the scriptures. If they don't want to read, they simply won't. This attitude is reflected in the lack of general reading activity among youth, which is typically limited to less than five minutes of their free time each day. Young members of the Church reflect this general trend as seen in the observations of seminary students.

Research conducted with seminary students also revealed that between 40 and 60 percent of all students cannot demonstrate an adequate understanding of the scriptures. The Mission Training Center has responded to this reality by providing special tutors who help young elders and sisters better understand what they read in the scriptures. Clearly we have a problem, as a number of faithful youth do not fully experience the blessings that come from reading and understanding the word of the Lord.

The realities of youth scripture reading present a challenge to parents who want their children to have the blessings that come from this activity. It is important for the family to provide a context that motivates youth to read and search the scriptures. This can happen in different ways, and the discussion that follows will help as you seek to encourage your youth to read the scriptures.

What to Do?

There are at least two different types of motivation. Intrinsic, or internal, motivation is related to a genuine interest in the scriptures and a desire to learn about them. The other type, extrinsic, is usually related to the rewards associated with competition or the avoidance of consequences for failure. This second type of motivation does little to encourage a lifelong love of reading and learning.

Intrinsically motivated scripture readers use their skills to read deeply because they are unsatisfied with a simplistic surface understanding. They search for new information and look for ways to apply it to their circumstances. They monitor their own understanding and adjust their reading skills to improve comprehension. The suggestions below are intended to help give youth this type of motivation.

These suggestions are also intended to promote "engagement," or active involvement in reading. Engaged readers have a purpose, a desired outcome, in mind. Readers who are not engaged tend to read mechanically, with little purpose. Parents should look for ways to help youth feel fully engaged in the adventure of scripture reading.

Basic Principles

Generally, telling teenagers what they ought to do simply doesn't work. Young people will read when they learn from their own experience the benefits of studying the scriptures. By following some basic principles, parents can help this happen.

Communication is at the heart of purposeful reading. Talking about the scriptures encourages young people to read the scriptures. Having an opinion, sharing an idea, or discussing a doctrine or principle—all are related to scripture reading. As we talk to our youth about the scriptures, we encourage them to read. The more interesting the conversation, the more motivated they will be to read and learn more.

Perhaps your family does not have much experience talking about the scriptures. If so, you may need to learn and practice together. This is not as difficult as you might think; our Church experiences provide a wealth of opportunity for family discussions. With a little effort, you can make the scriptures a part of many family conversations.

Such conversations can happen anytime, but you can also make them happen. For example, family home evening is a natural time for scripture discussions, as are mealtimes and informal parent interviews. You may find it effective to discuss a scriptural topic while driving alone with your youth, or during a quiet time before or after Church. You must be aware of your children's needs because you never know when the time may be just right for a scripture discussion.

One family encouraged scripture discussions with a question jar at the dinner table. As part of their scripture reading, they would write questions on slips of paper and put them into a jar. At dinnertime, one person would draw out a question for the family to discuss while eating.

Reading the scriptures should have a purpose. Youth respond best to purposeful activities that are immediate and concrete. Along with understanding why the scriptures should be read, youth also like to know what they can expect as a result of their reading.

When youth read with the purpose of doing something, they tend to read with increased understanding. For one family home evening, I decided to stage a news broadcast. Each family member received an assignment to play the part of a scripture character or a news reporter. As the family read the scripture selection, they prepared to play their roles. After our reading, the reporters carefully questioned the scripture characters and prepared their news reports. With the video camera rolling, each reporter made a thirty-second report.

The reading was purposeful, with a defined expectation and an opportunity for creative adaptation. The family enjoyed this scripture activity that greatly enhanced scripture understanding.

The home environment is important. Parents who read the scriptures during their free time provide an important model for their youth. Having a home library of books related to the scriptures is also important. A good Bible dictionary, one-volume commentaries, encyclopedias, and scripture-related novels all help young people expand their understanding and read more carefully and purposefully.

Giving books as gifts is one of our family traditions. Our children have received many with a scriptural theme. One of the most useful was a book we gave to our daughter, who was struggling with the Old Testament in seminary. It was a Bible storybook in a comic-book format that would appeal to youth. It was detailed and allowed our daughter to understand more fully what she read in the Old Testament. Seminary became more interesting when she was able to participate in class discussions.

Reading the scriptures is enjoyable. Youth need models who express their pleasure in reading the scriptures. Parents can provide this model by communicating the joy that comes from discovering an insight or understanding a difficult passage. Youth must know that parents who read the scriptures do feel the Spirit blessing their lives.

Our friend's family keeps a family scripture journal. As they read together, a family scribe summarizes the week's reading and adds personal notes. Drawings and other art are used to enhance the entry. Each family member takes turns writing in the journal. They take great pride in sharing the journal with others. It represents the heart of a rich family scripture tradition.

Reading the scriptures helps solve problems. Although the scriptures do not usually contain detailed answers to the specific challenges we face, they do invite the Spirit to help us understand what to do. Life becomes clearer and more understandable when we read the scriptures.

During a troubled time in our family, we prayed to know how to strengthen one of our teenage sons. We felt him slipping away and found that our efforts to help him became less effective. One night, after evening prayers, my wife shared her feeling that we needed to read the scriptures as a family. Because of a recent move and other circumstances, we had become lax in our usual practice. It had been easy to rationalize because the children were in seminary and we were all so busy trying to survive in our new community and job.

Responding to my wife's inspiration, we gathered our family and explained to them what Heavenly Father wanted us to do. They accepted, and we again set aside time each day to share an experience in the scriptures. After a month of reading together, we realized the positive effect of this simple family activity. We were grateful for the inspiration that nudged us to rearrange our priorities. Our son soon regained his enthusiasm for the gospel and again became interested in his family.

The scriptures help us understand our faith. In the Church we often explain our thoughts and ideas in terms of feelings. While this is valid, our faith also benefits from our intellectual understanding. Linking the heart and the mind makes sense in a Church that accepts intelligence as the glory of God.

Youth believe the gospel message because of the Spirit's influence, but this may not be enough as they face a confusing world. They need to combine the witness of the Spirit with a rational understanding of the gospel plan presented in the scriptures. New missionaries quickly discover that there are more questions than they can answer. This has the positive effect of encouraging them to search the scriptures and discover the rational foundation that underlies their faith.

All that we do in the Church has a scriptural basis.

When youth understand the scriptures, they discover why things happen as they do in the Church. Lessons become more interesting because they are able to follow discussion points and even contribute their own ideas and opinions. It is an exciting thing to understand the scriptures and have the ability to respond.

Ideas for Involving Youth

The following suggestions are designed to encourage youth to read and study the scriptures. As you consider these ideas, don't forget that motivating youth requires an appreciation of their unique needs and challenges. The basic principles discussed previously will help you select the best activities for your family.

Family home evenings. Giving youth responsibility for planning and teaching family home evening lessons gives them a definite purpose for studying the scriptures, an expected service as a result of their study, and an opportunity to share what they learn. Family nights are difficult for many families, as youth are busy with school and other activities. Nevertheless, it is important to maintain this tradition. Without it a family loses a valuable opportunity to help their youth grow.

Youth can prepare and present great family home evening lessons. The preparation helps them develop and practice scripture skills they will need later in missionary and family service. Remember that they are still learning and may need your help and support. The following guide is just a suggestion, but it illustrates the type of structure you can give youth to help them prepare effective, scripture-centered family home evenings.

1. *Pick a topic.* Picking a topic requires youth to study the scriptures and make decisions about what the family might need. They might:

a. consider a topic of family interest.

b. locate the topic in the Topical Guide.

c. read selected references from the Topical Guide and write down an idea from each one.

d. consider the resulting list of ideas and summarize them into a single main idea. This becomes the topic for the family home evening.

2. *Design a lesson.* Designing a lesson can be done in three parts. The first part requires the teacher to provide an activity that introduces the topic. The second part involves the family in learning from the scriptures. The third part concludes the lesson, with an opportunity for your youth to share their testimony of the truth of what was taught.

For example, in planning the lesson your youth might:

a. write the topic at the top of a piece of paper.

b. think of an activity, game, or object that represents the topic and could be used to introduce it.

c. give family members an opportunity to read from the scriptures to learn more about the topic.

3. *Teach the lesson.* The lesson should last less than thirty minutes, so the entire family home evening will take less than an hour. This time limit is important for families with youth who have homework and other demands on their time.

The young person teaching the lesson should:

a. follow the prepared lesson plan.

b. help every family member participate and contribute.

c. keep the lesson focused on the scriptures.

d. end the lesson with a personal testimony.

You can also buy idea books that will help your youth prepare effective lessons. Remember, however, that the goal is to give them opportunities to prepare and teach from the scriptures.

Scripture talks. In the Church we often have opportunities to speak in public. Too often youth simply read stories from various sources instead of giving scripture-based talks. This requires minimal effort and interest, and there is a better way.

The scriptures offer a wealth of ideas for great youth talks. Wise parents will guide young people to select a scripture topic for their presentation. This will require extra effort from the parents, but it will help youth grow in their ability to use the scriptures to teach the gospel.

As in preparing a family home evening, the Topical Guide is a useful starting point in preparing a talk. Young people can use it to find scriptures and information about a specific topic. They will need to read the references and write down key ideas they can use to organize their talk. As they organize the ideas, they may need help in writing a talk that does three things. First, it must capture the listeners' interest with a story, illustration, or example related to the selected topic. Second, it must provide insight based on scriptures related to the topic. Illustrations, stories, and examples are also helpful here. Finally, the talk needs to end with the youth's testimony of the truth taught in the scriptures. This is the most important part of the talk.

Remember the principles discussed earlier: Youth benefit from a clear purpose for studying the scriptures, a definite result from their studies, and an opportunity to share what they have learned. Preparing a scripture-based talk uses all three of these principles.

Personal scripture reading. Youth can explore the scriptures on their own with wonderful results. To encourage them, you will need to establish a home environment that gives them an opportunity to share what they are learning. You can encourage them to express themselves through their talents, such as music or art.

During a particularly challenging time, one of our sons often found himself at odds with his mother. He felt sad and withdrew into himself because of his challenges. Because our family had read the scriptures together for years, he found comfort in his personal reading of the scriptures. A breakthrough came at Christmas when he presented his mother with a pencil drawing of the Savior. Clearly, he had worked hours perfecting his drawing, which was his way of communicating his testimony and feelings during a difficult time in his life. The picture now occupies a place of honor in our living room.

Scripture journals are another way to encourage individual scripture reading. Many youth keep journals that record personal feelings and experiences. The scripture journal is an expansion of the personal journal as the youth records feelings, ideas, or impressions from reading the scriptures. This has the effect of encouraging the Spirit to witness the truthfulness of the scriptures. The scripture journal is an effective way to encourage personal scripture study.

Seminary. The single greatest influence outside the home on youth scripture reading is the seminary program of the Church. Wise parents complement the benefits of seminary with home experiences. Below are suggestions for doing that.

First, coordinate your family scripture reading with the topic being studied in seminary. Youth benefit from this extra emphasis on the scriptures and will appreciate your interest in seminary. If the seminary class is studying the Book of Mormon that year, then have your family also read that book together and focus on it during family home evening. This will reinforce what is being taught in seminary and give your teenager an opportunity to share what he or she is learning in class.

Next, meet the seminary teacher and ask for a tour of the classroom and an introduction to the program. The teacher will be happy to explain the wonderful program provided by the Church, including scripture mastery, reading expectations, and other special programs. As you learn about these things, you will be better able to magnify the seminary experience in your home. Family home evenings provide an excellent opportunity to give additional instruction on seminary topics. Youth also reinforce what they have learned in seminary by preparing and teaching lessons based on seminary discussions. These efforts will reinforce scripture learning and give youth a sense of accomplishment.

Summary

How can we ensure that our youth benefit from the scriptures? In a home that lacks a strong tradition of scripture reading, it is a challenge. You cannot encourage youth to do something that the family does not value or already practice. It is best when youth arrive at the teenage years having had a rich experience with the scriptures. If that is not the case, parents can start a tradition if they are committed to helping their youth use the scriptures in family home evening, in preparing talks, and in seminary. When this happens, the whole family benefits from the increased emphasis on the scriptures.

For families with a rich tradition of reading the scriptures, the suggestions in this chapter may further enhance individual scripture skills. Parents can expect growing independence in their teenagers' ability to use the scriptures in preparing lessons and serving in the Church.

In considering these things, it is important to remember a few basic ideas. Scripture activities must be purposeful. They should be related to service and should give youth an opportunity to communicate new knowledge and feelings. Your efforts to help will require patience and trust. If you insist that youth read scriptures for their own good, the benefits will be minimal. However, if you carefully plan meaningful experiences with the scriptures, you will encourage your youth to experience for themselves the blessings of our scripture heritage.

Activities for Teenagers

Continue the activities suggested in the previous section and explore those suggested below to broaden your children's understanding of the scriptures.

Activity	Purpose
1. Communication. Seek opportunities to discuss the scriptures. One way to do this is with a question jar at the dinner table.	Talking about the scriptures encourages youth to read and study them.
2. Purposeful reading. Encourage your youth to read with a definite purpose in mind. You might hold a news broadcast as a family home evening activity. Assign each member a role as a news reporter or a character from the scriptures, and have the reporters conduct an interview.	When reading activities have a definite expectation and provide an opportunity for creative adaptation, understanding of the scriptures increases.
3. Create a home library. Having a library of good books related to the scriptures is most beneficial. Encourage the use of Bible dictionaries, encyclopedias, and commentaries.	A library of supplementary books will provide useful insight and understanding to your youth as they seek to understand the scriptures.
4. Scripture talks. Encourage your youth to brainstorm talk ideas and then search for references in the Topical Guide. Teach them to end their talks by bearing their testimony.	Many benefits come from helping youth to share what they have worked hard to learn.
5. Scripture journals. A scripture journal is an expansion of a personal journal in which children are encouraged to record feelings, ideas, and impressions gained through diligent study of the scriptures.	Encourages the Spirit to witness the truthfulness of the scriptures.
6. Seminary. Your children's participation in this inspired program can be enhanced by encouraging your family to study along with your youth at home. Try to incorporate seminary lessons in family home evening activities.	Reinforces important seminary teachings and provides youth with a sense of accomplishment.

INdeX

Accountability, 42

Application, 31–32, 40

Art activities: during lap time, 24; during story time, 36–38, 40; during play time, 42, 53–55, 63, 64

Bedrooms: with scriptural-theme decorations, 21–22, 26; with bookshelves, 47–48

Book talk: during lap time, 20–21, 26; during story time, 30–31, 38, 40. See also Discussions, gospel-centered; Questions

Challenges to scripture study, 4–6

Characters in scripture stories, 32

Charts and graphs, 60

Children: learn of Heavenly Father, 4; different needs of, 5–6; developmental stages of, 8–12

Church magazines, 59

Collages, 54–55

Coloring books, 53

Commercial materials, 60–62, 64

Comparisons, 34, 40

Comprehension, scriptural, 2–3

Confidence, scriptural, 3

Contrasts, 34, 40

Craft activities, 54–55, 64

Cut-outs, 53

Discussions, gospel-centered: as aid in scripture study, 11, 31, 44–46, 62–63; in motivating youth, 71–72, 81. See also Book talk, Questions

Drama, 56, 63, 64

Echo reading (shadow reading), 50

Example, parents,' 52, 72–73, 79–80

Families, importance of, 3

Family home evening: as time for scripture study, 4–5, 10, 71; ideas for using scriptures during, 24, 26; giving youth responsibility for, 75–77

Family prayer, 59

Family scripture reading program: developing, 44–46, 74; journal of, 55, 73; scrapbook of, 55; reading activities during, 57–59, 64

Fantasy, 29, 30

Games, 10, 42

Gospel truths, reinforcing, 22, 27, 74

Group learning, 43

Homes, scripture-rich, 59–60, 72–73

Illustrations, 30, 50–51

Independence, 42–43

Interactive pictures, 51

Interpretation, 51

Interviews, 71

Intonation, 18

Journals, scripture, 55, 78, 81

Language development: begins at birth, 9, 7–18; through scripture-story time, 31; through word cards, 35–36

Language, scripture: introducing from birth, 9, 15–19, 23–25; during story-time age, 29; during play time, 44

Lap time: description of, 9, 13; scripture language development during, 15–19; ideas and activities during, 20–24

Lehi's Dream, 65–68

Library: home, 47, 64, 81; public, 48–49

Maps and charts, 51

Mealtimes, 71–72

Mini-dramas, 56–57
Missionary Training Center, 69–70
Mobiles, 22, 26
Motivation, 70–71
Music, 22, 26

News broadcast, 72, 81
Noah's ark, 20–21

Objects for reading activities, 57

Parenting, 12
Pictures, scriptural: for young
    children, 21, 23, 26; during story
    time, 33; as aid in retelling stories,
    35; for a month, 59
Play time: description of, 10, 13;
    reinforces learning, 41–42;
    increased skills of children during,
    42–45; asking questions during,
    45–47; independent reading
    during, 47–51; activities to use
    during, 52–61
Predicting, 32, 40, 46
Preparation, 45
Problem-solving, 33, 46, 73–74
Puppets, 37, 53

Question jar, 72
Questions: during story time, 28, 31;
    using inferential types of, 33, 40;
    uses of, for scripture study, 45–46,
    57–58; in helping youth learn
    better, 71–72
Quiet book, scripture, 21, 26

Reading, independent, 11
Reading activities, 57–59
Reading aloud: during lap time, 9, 16,
    26; during story time, 29, 31;
    during play time, 44, 50, 62, 64
Reading level, 30, 50
Reading skills, developing, 60–61
Repetition, 19, 27
Retelling, 34–35, 40
Rhythm, 18
Rocking chair, 15–16
Role playing, 56–57, 72

Sabbath Day, 22
Scrapbooks, scripture, 55
Scripture activity books, commercial,
    60–61
Scripture reading, personal, 78–79
Scripture reference game, 43
Scripture talks, 77, 81
Scriptures, personal, 22–23, 26
Scriptures, love for, 4
Seminary, 69–70, 78–79, 81
Signal word switch, 58
Silent dramas, 57
Skill books, 60
Slide shows, homemade, 56
Story time: description of, 9, 13,
    27–29, 38; ideas to use during,
    29–37
Storybooks, homemade, 54
Storybooks, scripture: importance of,
    9, 27–28; during lap time, 19–20,
    23–24, 26; during story time, 29;
    guidelines for choosing, 30,
    49–51; keeping a collection of, 48;
    from the public library, 48–49
Strips in a jar activity, 58

Teaching time: description of, 10, 13;
    encouraging teens during, 65–70;
    benefits of, 71–75; activities to use
    during, 75–79
Time management, 4–5
Topical Guide: for scripture study, 46,
    for Family Home Evening lessons,
    76–77; for scriptural talks, 77
Toys, scripture, 20–21, 26
Traditions, family, 51–52

Video productions, homemade, 56, 72
Videos, scriptural, 37–38, 40, 61–62
Vocabulary development: through
    scriptural storybooks, 30; through
    reading in context, 36, 40; during
    play time, 48–49

Word cards, 35, 59–60

Youth learners, 68–70